The Plan Was

A story about perseverance and promise

by Nadege J. Dady, Ed.D.

The Plan Was © Copyright 2023 Nadege Dady, Ed.D.

All rights reserved. No part of this publication may be reproduced, distributed, or transmitted in any form or by any means, including photocopying, recording, or other electronic or mechanical methods, without the prior written permission of the publisher, except in the case of brief quotations embodied in critical reviews and certain other noncommercial uses permitted by copyright law.

Although the author and publisher have made every effort to ensure that the information in this book was correct at press time, the author and publisher don't assume and hereby disclaim any liability to any party for any loss, damage, or disruption caused by errors or omissions, whether such errors or omissions result from negligence, accident, or any other cause.

Adherence to all applicable laws and regulations, including international, federal, state, and local governing professional licensing, business practices, advertising, and all other aspects of doing business in the US, Canada or any other jurisdiction is the sole responsibility of the reader and consumer.

Neither the author nor the publisher assumes any responsibility or liability whatsoever on behalf of the consumer or reader of this material. Any perceived slight of any individual or organization is purely unintentional.

The resources in this book are provided for informational purposes only and shouldn't be used to replace the specialized training and professional judgment of a health care or mental health care professional.

Neither the author nor the publisher can be held responsible for the use of the information provided within this book. Please always consult a trained professional before making any decision regarding treatment of yourself or others.

For more information, email ndady525@yahoo.com

ISBN: 979-8-88759-907-6 - paperback

ISBN: 979-8-88759-908-3 - ebook

Dedication

This book is dedicated to the planner in you.

*Like you, I love a good plan.
In fact, I find it thrilling to witness the outcome of a perfectly executed plan. Even more thrilling is the knowledge that it was achieved through hard work and personal effort.
As life loves to teach us, however, plans are best reserved for surprise birthday parties. The following stories, presented through equal parts tragedy and triumph, support the wisdom of altered plans.*

May you embrace your challenges and recognize them as ultimately part of your plan.

Table of Contents

Introduction 7

Chapter 1: The Plan Was to Go Away for College 9

Chapter 2: The Plan Was to Become a Pediatrician. 21

Chapter 3. 31

Chapter 4: The Plan Was to Accelerate My Professional Success. 35

Chapter 5: The Plan Was to Get Married and Have Children 41

Chapter 6: The Plan Was to Release My Ambitions 47

Chapter 7. 53

Chapter 8: The Plan Was to Live Life Quietly and Under the Radar. 61

Chapter 9. 65

Chapter 10. 69

Chapter 11: The Plan Was to Stop Making Plans 73

Acknowledgements 77

References 79

Author Biography. 81

Introduction

*A plan says, here is what I'm going to do and how I'm going to do it. It prepares you for the road ahead.
However, a good plan can only take you so far,
so you can make a plan B or C,
just in case something goes wrong.
Purpose works differently in our lives. It drives us forward regardless of what goes right or wrong.
Purpose says, here's the direction I'm going in,
no matter what obstacles get in the way or detours I encounter.
When we hold on to our plan,
we expect God to follow our idea of how things should work.
When we hold on to our purpose,
we surrender to the direction God wants to take us.*

-Unknown

Chapter 1

THE PLAN WAS TO GO AWAY FOR COLLEGE

"Miss, I'm sorry, but you're not eligible for financial aid," said the financial aid counselor. There was no warning. Shocked, I watched her lips move but couldn't fully comprehend her words in that moment. I stood there frozen. I imagined myself looking like a deer caught in headlights. A few seconds passed before I blurted, "But wait…what exactly does that mean?" She stood firm and looked at me with equal parts concern and familiarity with having to deliver this news often. Hesitant, the financial aid counselor repeated "I'm sorry but you're just not eligible for financial aid. I know that this is hard to hear, but it's true……." She had more to say, but I didn't hear much of it.

My mind floated elsewhere as I reflected on how I got here. I remembered fondly the day I decided that academics and a journey to college would be my route to success. One by one, I ruled out the options that wouldn't work. I enjoyed music but couldn't sing, at least not like any of the great singers of that era. I loved to dance but had only danced socially at the occasional party, not professionally. I was too petite for sports and hadn't really spent any time developing skills in that area or playing a sport long term. Acting seemed attractive too but also seemed out of reach. It became clear that pursuing a college degree would be my road to a hopeful future.

I suddenly refocused on the financial aid counselor. Her statement sounded definitive, as if a door had been permanently slammed shut. This was far from the truth, but it felt that way in that moment. I was an accepted student, but I wouldn't receive any financial aid for school. I would need to pay my way through college. Not understanding the process fully, my mother and I were convinced there was some sort of mistake. We traveled back to campus to discuss the matter with a different financial aid counselor. This time, there was more information. In the submission of my financial aid documents, the home that we lived in counted toward my mother's general assets and earnings. This equated to a portfolio that was below a certain level of financial need, which then automatically disqualified me for financial aid. We weren't prepared financially to pay out of pocket, so the reality of what I was up against suddenly set in. I might not be attending college that fall. All the joy I felt about starting school suddenly evaporated.

Paying out of pocket for school wasn't something we thought would be necessary. Given our financial portfolio,

The Plan Was

I would certainly qualify for financial aid, or so we thought. The truth about my portfolio, the house, my mother's earnings, and our collective financial portfolio was of course more complicated than that. My mom won ownership of the house from the divorce proceedings that my parents endured. The home, due to its age, was expensive to maintain. It was in constant need of repairs, which competed with her natural desire to save appropriately. We were living modestly and the emotional roller coaster between the divorce and the constant home repairs left us no time to prepare for college. I looked up and was suddenly getting ready for school. The irony, of course, was that the home was considered a significant asset in our financial portfolio and calculated into the bottom-line earnings, rather than the financial drain that it truly was. It would ultimately deduct from my opportunity to receive any financial aid at all.

To be clear, I'm grateful for the comfortable home environment that I grew up in. It took perseverance, effort, and strategic juggling to maintain our stable environment through years of conservative financial decision making. My mom thought it important to acquire the home for a few other reasons. First, the location was family friendly. My school schedule, network of friends, and access to extended family visits would remain uninterrupted. Secondly, it meant she could raise her only daughter in a safe neighborhood. The issue of safety was paramount to her during those development years, as a divorced woman raising an only child in New York City. The focus on safety took on many forms in our household and incorporated discussions on traveling to and from school, taking public transportation, the importance of curfew, and the occasional chaperoned social event. This focus on safety later expanded to the need for me to stay local for college, local as in New York City. At the time, there were widespread concerns about college campus life away from home. Stories of students experiencing difficulty, engaging in too many extracurricular activities that distracted them from reaching the goal of graduation permeated her social network and our discussions. Finally, we arrived at a conclusion, me defiantly, her assertively, that the best plan was for me to stay local for college.

There would be one more meeting with another financial aid counselor before we landed in the office of the Dean of Student Affairs. The interactions with him left a lasting positive impression on me about the powerful role that an administrator can have on a student. He was dynamic, energetic, and very positive. More importantly, he was undaunted by this news we were grappling with as a family. He discussed my options and even came up with an alternate plan. In the immediate timeframe, I would take an emergency loan to cover the first semester, and then work part time on campus to pay back the loan. The plan moving forward was to continue working each semester on campus to cover tuition as well as personal expenses. The solution arrived just as quickly as the problem had presented itself. I was officially back in action as an accepted college student. Despite the initial disappointment of not being able to move away for college, I embraced my new life. I traveled to and from campus by commuting on the NYC transit system. I had no idea what to expect, but I found my new environment on campus to be very exciting. Growing up in a sheltered environment, I attended an all-girls Catholic high school as well as a Catholic grammar school. In contrast college campus life was diverse and co-ed with tons of activities to do and new people to meet. The depth of diversity on campus shocked me, meeting people from all walks of life, including international students. The campus and curriculum seemed so expansive I exhausted myself every day from the newness of it all. I was never short of enthusiasm or optimism for the next day. I absolutely loved it. With such a positive turn of events, I finally felt comfortable to think about my next steps: identify a major and choose a career path. I would become a physician I thought, a pediatrician to be exact.

Having set my sights on pursuing a career in medicine, I scheduled my first visit with the college's premed advisor about three months after I started classes. I found his demeanor interesting, quite opposite to that of the Dean of Student Affairs. He said very little and was conservative and observant. I ignored my instincts and decided to not allow this initial impression to deter me; I was only gathering information at this point. He went on to share the list of classes, the deadlines, and requirements that I would need to meet over the next three years in order to successfully apply to medical school. It was all-consuming, and despite the gut feelings I had about his guidance, I was very excited to be on this journey. I envisioned the end goal, however distant it still was. I was also surrounded by other students who had the same goals, so it energized my feelings about the future.

The next few months consisted of a rigorous work and school schedule; an hour commute to school followed by early morning classes that would start at 8AM. I would work for a few hours during the day, followed by evening classes that would end at 8PM, then an hour commute back home for two days of the week. The other two/three days consisted of relatively the same schedule with a substitution of study time in the library during the day for work. For the entire four years this was my schedule with slight variations in between. It was grueling but didn't feel that way because I was optimistic about my life trajectory. This optimism even led me to register as a premed student with the premed advising office. As a declared premed student, the office was responsible for monitoring my progress in the required courses. These courses are a list of mostly science courses that count toward your application to medical school. Performance in those courses feeds the recommendation letters that are prepared by the premed advisor in support of your application. The office would receive periodic updates on my academic progress as well as copies of published transcripts. Having overcome the initial financial aid hurdle to start school made me feel like all I had to do to obtain my goal was work hard. Success therefore was basically assured, since things had fallen into place so nicely. Soon, however, the reality of what I had signed up for set in. The grueling schedule that I had carved out for myself was, in fact, too exhausting. The end of the school year had arrived, it was final exam week, and I was stressed. My first semester performance in the premed courses wasn't my best. My plan of action was to turn that around and finish strong by over performing during final exam week in the second semester. The stakes were now higher than ever before as a declared premed student.

As summer arrived, I continued to work on campus and patiently waited for the announcement that transcripts would be released. I was sure that I had met my goals because of all the time and effort I had put into organizing my workload and studying for each exam. One day, confirmation arrived; official transcripts were published and mailed home. When I got home from work, I took a seat at the kitchen table and reviewed the contents of my transcript slowly. The grades that I received in the required liberal arts courses, as well as my declared major courses were excellent. The grades I received in my premed courses, however, were a personal disappointment. Crushed, I sat there reflecting on what could have possibly gone wrong. I was an honors student in high school. I graduated at the top of my class and did so well that I earned a scholarship. I was picked to deliver the class speech at graduation. I was used to being a top performer and now this. Wasn't I the same excellent performing student from high school? My optimism wouldn't save me from this reality. I was struggling with how to process it all. Nonetheless, it was a confusing turn of events; I had achieved excellent grades in the non-pre-med courses, so they produced a respectable academic average. I knew however that it was just as important to demonstrate that same excellence in the premed courses. As a declared premed major, everything was dependent on this. I was concerned but I was also so used to achieving on my own that the thought of seeking assistance never even crossed my mind.

The pursuit of a career in medicine is indeed highly competitive. As I contemplated the start of the new school year, I had questions but mainly for myself. What would I do differently this year to ensure a more successful outcome? I was in deep denial about my challenges and found it almost impossible to accept what had happened in the first academic year. I convinced myself that all I needed was to just put forth more effort. I did what came naturally and leaned into a positive frame of mind in preparing to tackle the next academic year. I devised a plan to retake those premed courses, achieve better grades and demonstrate my ability to improve to the premed advisor. I scheduled an in-person meeting with him and explained that the first academic year didn't reflect my potential and I was ready to tackle my studies with more hard work. Again, his demeanor was quiet, reserved, and observant. No strategies for success, no referrals to academic support, just observant. I continued to ignore my instincts about him and attributed his lack of enthusiasm to his inability to recognize my potential. I was certain he would act differently once he saw me turn my academic performance around. There was only one problem with my "new" plan. It wasn't "new" at all; I kept the exact same study habits, same work schedule, and didn't change anything about how I approached my studies. So, it might surprise you to learn, sarcasm intended, that my performance in those premed courses produced the exact same results as the year prior. It certainly surprised me. The follow up visit with the premed advisor was just depressing. He was unflinching in his analysis and evaluation; I wouldn't be competitive in my medical school applications. "Think of another direction, because, at this point, this is just a waste of your time," he said. As sad as I was about his observations, we respectfully agreed to disagree. Deplete of options, as I exited the meeting, I stumbled upon a flyer for a science tutor outside his office. At this point, my instincts were screaming at me to do something different, so I grabbed a copy. As I looked up briefly, I noticed two other students in the lobby of the office. My eyes made contact with one of the other students. He asked me, "How did your meeting go with him, just curious?" Feeling defeated in that moment, I replied, "Not that great." He responded immediately, "That's typically how his meetings tend to go with people like us" as he touched the back of his hand to highlight our shared dark complexions. I heard him loud and clear; he felt that our negative experiences with the advisor were due to our race. Mentally, I drifted away momentarily to reflect on this revelation. First, my instincts were waving red flags all along. The advisor emanated a cold demeanor in all of our interactions. The type of demeanor that indicated he had already sized me up as well as my potential. This, as opposed to someone waiting to discover my potential through what I would demonstrate or through our personal interactions and conversations. In hindsight, I can tell you there is a significantly important difference in the approach, especially from someone in a powerful advisory role such as this. Secondly, I had no idea other students in the program felt this way. My intense focus on strengthening my performance in the sciences left me no time to seek out my peers. The thought that an advisor, who is paid to provide guidance and support, would actively seek to be unsupportive gave me pause. But truth can, at times, be stranger than fiction and is a candid reality faced by students of color. As I refocused on our discussion, I looked up at him one more time and thanked him for sharing before I exited the lobby. As I left, he said, "Be careful with him." Though I accepted what my peer shared with me, I was now more convinced than ever before that my potential for success was going to be up to me. I didn't waste any more time and called the tutor immediately. I found him to be very nice and inviting. He gave me all the necessary information and provided me with scheduled dates, times, and the cost for attending these sessions. I decided this was worth it; I would reallocate the necessary funds to cover this. To me, it was clear and simple; I desired a different outcome, so I would need to dedicate the time and resources to do so. I arrived at my first tutoring session and unlocked a door of wonder. Surprisingly, the room was packed. They were all there, all of my classmates, the same ones who excelled at each exam, who always knew the material, front row and center, fully engaged with the tutor.

This was a major turning point, and, although easier to reflect on in hindsight, the problem was that I had a hard time facing my challenges. The answer was always there waiting for me; I had simply delayed its arrival. If I had only accepted the facts, I might have pursued a different solution sooner, causing less stress to my journey. I delayed facing my disappointments head on, which also delayed opportunities for discovering more appropriate, winning strategies. The other poignant lesson here is that life's disappointments aren't fixed outcomes. There is always a solution; you just have to find it.

Chapter 2

THE PLAN WAS TO BECOME A PEDIATRICIAN

Performance in my premed courses had now improved. I was more satisfied with my learning strategies and felt at home with the content. I continued to juggle work, commuting to school, and studying. The stress and intensity of my first two years started to dissipate but the impact on my transcript would linger. As a declared premed major, the third year of college is divided between preparing your application to medical school and taking the Medical College Admission Test (MCAT). The fourth year of college is reserved for traveling to medical school interviews. I started the third year and felt ready to tackle what lay ahead, despite not knowing anything about MCAT prep courses or anything at all about how to successfully maneuver through the process. Much like the discovery I made about my classmates who had been working with the tutor/learning specialist to arrive at the outcomes they desired. I would later discover, after the fact that there was a similar process for taking prep courses prior to taking the MCAT. These courses are specially designed as learning strategies to assist with how to take the test and get the best possible outcome. They don't enhance the content that the test taker has learned; rather, they assist with time-saving strategies for answering all questions, a key component of excelling on the exam. This is an important factor in mastering the exam because it's timed. There's a cost associated with taking such a prep course, but it's much like the cost associated with the tutor; it's worth it for the purpose of achieving the goal. Without any of this knowledge, I scheduled the MCAT exam and waited for the confirmation in the mail. Meanwhile I gathered my recommendation letters from the faculty I had developed rapport with. Unexpectedly, the MCAT examination date, which was scheduled and paid for in advance, would conflict with a childhood friend's wedding date. The exam would take all day, 9AM-5PM, leaving me no room to complete the exam and make it to her wedding, which was scheduled to start at 11AM. Thankfully, within the larger network of our friends were others who had previously taken the MCAT. With their prior experience, they confirmed the difficulties of sitting for an all-day exam. Our friendship survived the disappointment of my absence, and we are still friends to this day. It was, nonetheless, one of the earliest lessons I learned about how personal sacrifice is, at times, the cost for committing to the pursuit of one's goals.

The date of the MCAT exam had arrived and I packed a bag filled with snacks. It was an eight-hour paper-based exam, and I was going to need endurance to focus through the day. After completing the exam, I felt confident and more hopeful than ever before. As I awaited the results of the MCAT, I continued collecting recommendation letters and scored an exciting volunteer opportunity at a local hospital. The hospital setting was always brimming with activity; they had a large cohort of Haitian immigrant patients. My job was to translate between doctor and patient. I would translate from Haitian-creole to English and vice versa. It felt like a wonderful way to give back and learn about the hospital setting from a more intimate perspective. The doctors, hospital staff, and patients were all very appreciative and sought to support my future goals. In the meantime, I researched the medical schools in the tristate area. Without the knowledge of a need for a strategy even at the application phase, I would apply only to a handful of schools, the most competitive ones in the area. I continued to ignore my premed advisor, whom I now perceived as persistently discouraging each time I visited his office to complete my premed portfolio. I patiently waited for the arrival of the MCAT score report. A few members of my class who took the exam around the same time that I did had already received their scores. I started to get nervous, so I called the testing center to follow up; I wanted to make sure that they had the right name and address. I was delighted when the phone attendant said, "Your MCAT scores are in the mail." A few days later, I arrived home to find the letter waiting for me on the dining room table. My future was waiting; all I had to do was open the envelope.

I opened the envelope to a collection of MCAT scores that were disappointing. They wouldn't meet the threshold for a competitive application. Had the premed advisor been right all along? What on earth was going on with me? Had my previous academic successes been a figment of my imagination? What about all the time and work that I had put into the tutor sessions? While the answers to those questions continued to play loudly in my mind, I stared at the scores one last time and decided, with surprising ease, that medicine was just not for me. The combination of no prior knowledge of the need for an MCAT prep course, the need for a strategy when applying to schools that might be searching for a student like me, the ability to retake the MCAT, my initial lackluster performance in the premed courses, and the premed advisor's persistent discouragement of my efforts eventually drowned out my desires. It felt liberating and, at the same time, strange to simply let it go. So much time had already been invested, so many social activities sacrificed in pursuit of this goal. I was surprised by my apparent ease in accepting this change of direction. I shifted my energy quickly to work on a communication plan. Who would I inform first, my parents? Or should I first tell my friends who had seen little of me during those years due to all of that studying? How would my premed advisor, who had been negative about this all along, react? It was transformative, but not as awful as I thought it was going to be. I just announced it to everyone; they accepted it, and life moved on.

Despite the disappointing change in direction, the end of my senior year in college was littered with happy, uplifting moments. I felt accomplished nonetheless; graduating with my bachelor's degree meant that I was closing that chapter in my life. The entire family would attend the graduation ceremony, which brought us together to celebrate. Following graduation, I focused on further developing my relationship with my boyfriend. We would travel twice a year and create more time for joy, which helped me to rest from all those years of grueling work and school schedule. I was now also entering the professional world as a full-time employee. As I continued to enjoy my new normal, which was filled with less stress, more time for fun, family, and friends as well as travel, I tried my best to forget the past. Once in a while, I found myself intimidated by the fact that I had no idea what I was going to do next. The only thing I was certain about was that I wanted to continue my education. Medicine used to be the plan, but no longer. As I was searching for full-time work, I continued to work part time on campus. One day, a colleague visited to deliver the news that she would be applying to a graduate program. We weren't particularly close; we had just worked in the same department through the years and had developed a friendly rapport. We had both graduated and were figuring out next steps. She shared that applying to the program would be a great way to continue the academic journey beyond the bachelor's degree and invited me to apply with her. She even suggested that we should work on submitting our applications together to keep each other accountable. To this day, I have no idea why she chose to share her thoughts with me, or why she felt so compelled that we would pursue this together to keep each other accountable. I simply agreed to what seemed like a plan with perfect timing.

It was an intense summer of job searches, but I finally landed a job at a small sales office. I was charged with supporting the sales representatives who needed to negotiate with or acquire new clients every day. I did really well. I did so well, in fact, the president informed me he would soon promote me. I reflected on how much of a great opportunity this was. I was making great money for someone still living at home who just graduated college. But I wondered where this opportunity was leading me careerwise. I had no formal training in finance or sales. So, what exactly would he promote me to? I didn't see a clear way forward nor did I understand its connection to anything that I had any long-term interest in. Something about it never felt permanent. Six months later, the company experienced extreme financial difficulties and, since I was the most recent hire in the office, I was the first one fired. I spent three months that summer looking for work with absolutely no success. I was living at home, with no income and feeling overwhelmingly defeated. Life wasn't making any sense. "What was I really good at? Did I know? If not, how was I going to discover it?" Medicine felt right, I really wanted to be a Pediatrician. Now that goal seemed farther away than ever. I felt derailed and defeated.

I took time to consider what attracted me to medicine and discovered that I had a profound need to be useful. It also became apparent that I had a need to use my overactive mental energy for good. I could easily analyze and dissect situations for hours, so I knew that I needed to structure that gift wisely. I had also developed a certain perception about adulthood. I characterized it as filled with never-ending responsibility, disappointment, and difficulty and decided that I needed a career. I wanted to keep engaged in the mental process of contributing to society. Though I wrestled with these feelings for years, they were difficult to articulate to my loved ones. No one knew about this inner struggle. In their presence, I projected a laid-back attitude to life's shifting challenges. Spending time alone and in deep thought would help me organize my thoughts and emotions. It took me three months to secure a new job. It wasn't my first choice, but it was finally income. I served as a junior accountant in a stocks and bonds trading firm for exactly one day. It wasn't for me. The office was cold, the orientation was cold, and I just couldn't imagine being productive in that setting. That same day, I was also hired by a nonprofit, healthcare/public health agency. It was a much better match for my long-term interests. This new environment was warm and felt like home. The company placed a high value on education, research, teaching, and continuous development. They were looking for someone dependable and responsible, and I was looking for opportunities to exercise my intellectual curiosity. We met each other's needs. I started in an administrative position but that didn't matter to me at all. The organization was attractive because of the range of public health care topics that I was exposed to. I was like a sponge and took every opportunity to learn. As I built my trust in the organization and them in me, I was eventually given more responsibility. Not only was I good at the organizational tasks I was responsible for, but I also enjoyed them. Free thought was encouraged; participation in organizational activities and, most importantly, my feedback on critical issues were sought after. The more I did, the more responsibilities I was given. Around this time, I also received confirmation that I was accepted into the graduate program I had applied for with my friend. I would work full time while pursuing my graduate degree. Sensitive to the needs of its working students, the program provided an intensive curriculum that incorporated all-day Saturday classes with evening courses disbursed throughout. Meanwhile, my responsibilities at work grew exponentially. I would now be required to not only supervise students but to teach them as well.

At last, life was starting to make sense again. The more I explored public health topics, the more I learned that there were many issues to solve. Those issues needed solutions and I had awakened to the fact that I might be able to contribute in meaningful ways. I could indeed be useful, aligning my gifts and using creativity to contribute positively to our society. I was inspired and, for the first time in a long time, feeling hopeful again. The range of responsibilities that I was charged with pushed me beyond my comfort zone and, for this, I will forever be thankful. I attended conferences, training seminars, anything that helped me to finesse my skills and learn new ones. I would do research, prepare, and deliver content to groups of individuals that would have intimidated me just a few years prior. It felt extremely important to be engaged in the work I was doing, and I came to appreciate how important it was to remain intellectually curious. These challenges seemed custom made for me. Creativity in particular, made me a stronger administrator, as I consistently trusted my instincts to find answers. In the practical sense, the places where projects tended to stall were the exact places I could contribute with a creative solution. It was the perfect marriage.

Chapter 3

To my surprise, creativity led me to opportunities to manage programs focused on exposing students who were underrepresented in medicine (URiM) to the health professions. The Association of American Medical Colleges (AAMC) defines underrepresentation in medicine relative to representation in the US population, and are categorized as Black, Latino, Native American and Asian Pacific Islander.[1] Critical to the success of this project was the ability to identify appropriate resources and link students to mentors who could properly advise them. *What an interesting twist of events,* I thought. Not too long ago, I was one of those students. Yet, I would be placed in a position to link students to appropriate mentors in the healthcare professions. I took on this particular assignment with great enthusiasm. The irony of becoming exactly the type of resource I would have searched for as a student consistently played in my mind. I thought it an honor to find ways to encourage students who looked like me and experienced the same barriers to success as I did. I would later embrace this as my higher calling and what I had been in search of all along. In the meantime, I continued to focus on the need to complete the master's program that I was fully enrolled in. Experiencing graduate school as a full-time working professional was much different than as a full-time student in an undergraduate college. I was going to school all day Saturday as well as one night after work during the week. There were some other additional first-time life experiences also happening at that time. I was living on my own, paying my own bills, and balancing my own check books. Professionally, the tasks at work supported what I was learning in school, so there was a nice relationship between what I was learning and how I implemented them in daily practice. I was also paying more attention to how I made important decisions by ensuring that I did prior research and considered all options before arriving at a final decision. Everything was falling into place and felt more concrete than ever before.

This would also be a transformative time for committing to lifelong learning and furthering self-improvement. As a part of the graduate academic program, I was required to take a writing course that met in the evenings throughout the semester. The professor was an older gentleman, who erred more on the side of telling the unfiltered truth, no matter how it landed on the perception of the receiver. He was concerned about my writing. Each assignment was returned with a list of issues that needed correction. In stark contrast with regard to style, one day a colleague approached me to suggest that I improve my writing skills if only to support the increasing greater responsibilities and visibility that I was experiencing at work. She was wonderfully skilled at delivering this sensitive message while also connecting it to the upside of my exponential growth. She understood that my responsibilities at work required that I send more professional correspondence within our network, which meant that my writing was increasingly visible to various members of our organization through email, memos, letters, or special notifications. As she demonstrated the value of this timely opportunity for growth, I responded to her selfless act of generosity by immediately crafting an action plan. Following our discussions, I contemplated the importance of constructive feedback in our lives. Children are often protected from critique to allow them the room to grow through trial and error. As adults, however, honest communication with those you trust becomes critical to success, growth, and personal development. Responsible adults do their best to not take these conversations personally, even if the truth doesn't align with how they see themselves. I decided that I would do what was necessary to improve. My colleague assisted in identifying a continuing business education course focused on the tenants of business writing. It was free, offered a flexible schedule, and even provided continuing education credit for participation. I also attended one-on-one meetings with the English professor to better understand where I was falling short. I had implemented the necessary changes and, within weeks, started to enjoy the results of my efforts. It had an incredible unforeseen but positive impact on my confidence and self-esteem. I achieved a high grade in the course and my colleague was now complimenting me regularly about what she saw as a vast improvement in my writing style. The importance of this lesson is that writing is an extension of who we are and how we show up in the world, whether that be through letters, personal notes, memos, emails, and now, social media. Our writing provides clarity on a topic, which is an extension of the clarity of our thoughts around said topic. Clear thought leads to clear processes, which support the ability to accomplish our goals. Our writing, therefore, is an extension of the clarity we have with ourselves, our constituents, employers, colleagues, family, friends, partners, etc. Without this clarity, the reader will lose interest quickly.

Often, I think of the English professor and my former colleague, feeling grateful for this ever-evolving gift. It was a great investment in my development, and I felt satisfied with the results. I eventually felt comfortable enough to let myself fall in love with writing and exploring its different styles, thinking that it might one day serve me in creative ways.

Chapter 4

The Plan Was to Accelerate My Professional Success

Several years later, I had completed my master's degree program as well as some important professional milestones. With a few years of productivity under my belt, I was now seeking greater financial and professional growth. I would later leave the company that I had come to consider a safe and comfortable environment. I took a position at another organization that I thought would better align with more pressing needs. As I settled into the new role, I planned to engage in the type of development that I thought would fast track professional successes. As an example, there was an opportunity to learn more about research and its role in forming national policy-level decisions. Without research or the systematic investigation into the study of subjects, it would be very difficult to establish facts and/or reach new conclusions. There are also preexisting rules for engaging in research and how to successfully conduct it. The more I learned, however, the more I discovered how much more there was to learn. What became clear in this new path was that the learning curve was steep and required greater skill to handle people as opposed to projects, meaning I was going to need a deeper understanding of the emotional landscape of others while balancing my own. I thought myself to be well-prepared for the challenge and moved forward with great intent.

As my professional role expanded and I learned the nuances of the new environment, I felt like a kid in a candy store. Everything seemed brightly lit with wonder and possibility. I was proud of myself for stepping outside of my comfort zone and taking one more leap toward my goals. Other personal exciting moments were part of this transition too such as learning how to drive and purchasing my first car. I spent most of my undergraduate college years reliant on the New York City public transportation system. So, to now drive everywhere felt like freedom. I also transitioned out of the environment that I grew up in and moved to a completely different zip code. As I adjusted to all the newness, I had very little time to prepare for or evaluate the inconsistencies in the new environment. I was already here and already expected to perform. I learned daily about the importance of asking the right questions. Conversely, asking the wrong questions fills the space of silence; keeps the conversation going without ever really getting to the heart of the matter. What is optimal about practicing deeper listening is that the nuances of human interactions inform our next steps. When you have heard someone thoroughly through active listening, the "right" questions are then easier to form. Through this I discovered that I had been only listening to provide a response and that there was, in fact, a distinct and important difference between where I was and where I wanted to go. Professionally, if success in your environment is defined by how well you understand the dynamic, you understand that asking the right questions becomes a critical part of that success. Excelling in my career, therefore, would mean leaning into this new skill and embracing a vastly different approach to what I was accustomed to. The more I leaned into this newly developed skill set, however, the more I encountered a variety of confusing and difficult experiences that seemed illogical. Each experience made me feel out of place and like I simply didn't belong there. Ironically, I conducted research on the topic only to discover the academic term to describe what I was feeling. Belonging Uncertainty Theory[2,3] is an internalized dialogue that replays itself in your mind and sounds like, "I don't think I belong here." Also referred to as imposter syndrome, this internal dialogue complicates the ability to form trusting relationships that are needed for success. Social belonging, the ability to see oneself as connected, is understood to be a basic human need.[4,5] Therefore, when people feel socially connected it predicts favorable outcomes on their mental and physical well-being.[2,3] In the context of a professional environment, when people feel socially integrated, they experience less discomfort[6], are better able to form trusting relationships, and take advantage of what the environment has to offer[7,8,9]. Following this important discovery in researching the topic and reflecting on the difficult experiences I had encountered, I came to understand that the reason they felt so incredibly challenging was because I didn't feel like I belonged. In fact, I regularly experienced quite the opposite. One such example was when I was falsely accused of causing the failure of a project that I wasn't even involved in. I was cleared, of course, because there was no evidence to prove what I had been accused of. I consider myself fortunate that another colleague quickly jumped in to clear up the confusion about my misperceived involvement. The experience would forever leave a lasting impression, as I wondered about the potential impact on professional reputation and financial stability. I had accrued school loans, moved to a different zip code, and even bought a car, all in the name of adjusting to the new environment and working toward greater professional success. I was disappointed that it had come to this, and the interactions with the accusing individual, unfortunately, didn't stop there. My internal dialogue of feeling like I didn't belong grew more intense as they felt it necessary to remind me of "my place" in the hierarchy of the organization. Upset by the fact that I had been cleared of their false accusation, they immediately summoned me to their office. The meeting was impromptu and had no context. Although I now didn't feel comfortable in their presence, I went anyway because they were higher in rank. They abruptly asked me to enter their office. As I entered the room, they announced, "Just remember that you're the low man on the totem pole." Stunned by the comment, I stood there for a few seconds reactionless. Sensing that this was the entire point of the meeting, I promptly exited the room and went back to my office. The attack was unprovoked and unsolicited; I felt threatened. I started to question what led to such a strong reaction from this person. From my perspective, I posed no threat; I wasn't even a direct report to them. I suddenly grew concerned about what other experiences might follow. A few months later, the individual would leave the program, temporarily alleviating me of some sleepless nights, but the damage was already done. I was now awakened to the nuances of human frailty. I don't recall what my expectations were or why, but up until that incident, I believed that professional environments were safe spaces. I was terribly wrong about that, but I offer an examination of my history for greater understanding. I grew up in a sheltered environment where lies had serious consequences. There was a strict moral code, and I grew up thinking that this was universally shared. Through this experience, I learned that although we are all human and have the same human needs for love, security, recognition and validation, our approaches to getting our needs met can be vastly different. I didn't understand that for some, any means could potentially be used to gain an advantage. Yet, I would repeatedly encounter these experiences in others. As hard as those lessons were, they taught me to operate with others from a more sober, attentive, and active listening perspective. I now started to really pay attention to others and what they revealed about themselves. I came to accept the fact that my plans to accelerate my success couldn't be realized in this environment. Not in the ways that I had dreamed of and embraced the clarity about this particular journey. Developing greater trust in myself would prove difficult but my new plan was to simply learn as much as I could as I grew to distrust the environment. As it relates to imposter syndrome, confidence is much easier to project when your childhood experiences nurture your confidence and you feel comfortable in your own skin, irrespective of the environment or the other players in the sandbox. It's far more difficult to project confidence when you have experienced challenges that are anxiety provoking and must be unlearned.

    I withdrew emotionally from the experiences that were causing me unnecessary pain and confusion. I had a greater need to activate my faith and lean on a higher power. Prayer, meditation, reading, and self-reflection sustained me during this timeframe. To escape the disappointment, I turned my attention to my personal life.

Chapter 5

THE PLAN WAS TO GET MARRIED AND HAVE CHILDREN

One of the more serious relationships I had was when I was a senior in college lasted a number of years, and we even lived together for some of those years. He was a good person, with a solid character and strong family values. By the time we graduated from college, he was ready for marriage, but I felt ill prepared. Growing up so sheltered, I didn't know anything about life outside of the school environment. I thought it important to understand how to financially support myself and learn a little bit more about the world. Thus, we would eventually go our separate ways. Returning to this moment in my journey, I was now living on my own and experiencing life through an adult lens. At last, I was feeling more financially independent and decided the time was right to open myself up to love, as the thought of getting married and having kids was now front and center in my mind.

I could hardly believe that I met him. He appeared before me as the embodiment of all that I had prayed for in a soul mate. Falling for him felt so sweet and natural. I recall how overwhelmed I got when I contemplated the thought of our potential for "Big Love." On the surface, he met all of my needs. In my mind, I had already planned the wedding, the home we would live in, and the neighborhood where we would settle and have children. I even dreamt about the professional projects we would work on together, we seemed to be that aligned in our goals and destined to be together. But I spent so much time dreaming about our potential life together, I didn't pay attention to his character. It's really funny how crystal clear it is when you're reflecting back on it. From the most naïve and innocent space, I romanticized the entire relationship. He flirted to gain my attention and projected an air of shy innocence, always hesitant and careful about his delivery. I found that very flattering and so I obliged. The timing was so perfect; only God could have orchestrated this union. He was single with no children, and so was I. Everything about our union made sense, including the mutual attraction I thought I sensed. Although I also understood that we differed in our upbringing I decided to roll with the punches. Whatever I didn't know, I would get from books focused on building effective relationship dynamics and long-lasting fulfilling unions. I was sincere in my beliefs and trusted the plan that was emerging before me. I was going to marry my soul mate. Emotionally, I had placed a great deal of faith in a situation that provided me with no reliable proof for trusting it.

It's painful to revisit this many years later, but some context is needed to better understand the thought patterns of a much younger me. My exposure to men in my formative years was to my father, grandfather, as well as a handful of uncles and cousins. They were the type of men who were stable, honest, hardworking, protective, and very loving toward their family, not perfect, just loving. This shaped what I came to expect from love and relationships. I was about nine years old when my parents divorced. Life immediately became financially insecure and unfolded quickly. Extended family played a stabilizing role, but, with each passing year, the stress and strain of the divorce became more pronounced. The adjustments we had to make after the divorce forever left an impression. What was clear to me even at nine years old, especially as it relates to the impact of marriage on women, was that a woman's happiness and security is tied to a husband's ability to provide. Consequently, her happiness significantly diminishes with his absence. I would plan a future that would be the exact opposite. I would become financially independent before I gave myself over to love, embark on marriage, or have children. I would wait for a time when I could also contribute to a stable household before opening myself to love.

So, when what I thought was love presented itself, I believed it to be divinely inspired. I gave myself freely and approached it with naïve trust, even though we appeared to be from different worlds and not quite equally yoked. As I critically reflect, I remember being forewarned about him. "Don't go there; he's trouble" said one eager onlooker. I dismissed the warnings because I didn't trust the source. I saw it as an unsupportive critique of someone just trying to do their best. The truth, however, landed like the sharp edges of a sword, cutting through what I wouldn't allow myself to see. The ugly truth was that he was neither innocent nor shy, nor was he intent on giving me his best. He didn't think twice about deceiving me and then bragged about it to those who took an interest in what might be developing. Though I wasn't looking for any red flags, they were there. I sometimes got the sense that he resented me for believing in him, in us, and our potential love. There was also something about the way he would stare at me, like he was secretly making fun of how naïve I was in that moment. It forever shifted my understanding and expectations about love. To put it plainly, this was an extremely painful and lonely experience. I didn't share the details of what happened with anyone, so no one knew the extreme depth of my sadness, not even my family. I was ashamed, disgusted, and, by now, a master at hiding my emotions. To the outside world, I had moved on. But it took longer than anyone knew to get back to my old self because this experience wasn't like any other experience I had ever had. It called into question the trust that I extended to others. I came to understand that most people mask deep layers of internal conflict. When you sense a lack of transparency, it's your responsibility to find out how that internal conflict shows up in their interactions with you. With this understanding, I granted myself the grace I needed to heal from the devastation. I acknowledge the fact that nothing had prepared me for this experience, so I simply had to go through it in order to make it to the other side.

I was so moved by the disappointment of this failed relationship that after two years of repeatedly confronting my sadness, I simply let it go. Perceiving myself to be healed and moving on from the emotional wreckage, I didn't ever expect to see him again. One day, he visited unannounced. There was no context or reason for this surprise visit; he appeared just as he had disappeared many years ago. He felt it necessary to relay the news, in person, that he was now a married man. Interestingly, he shared the news with a look of awkward disassociation from the obvious weight of the message and attempted to further minimize its importance through humorous gesturing. In that moment, I saw him for who he truly was. He was neither my soul mate nor my friend. Wiser now, I sensed this was nothing more than a ploy to gauge a reaction, so I instinctively smiled. I congratulated him, wished him well on his journey, and exited the premises as fast as I could. I cried the entire way home.

Chapter 6

The Plan Was to Release My Ambitions

Exhausted by all of the emotional turmoil, I felt inspired to take control of my future. Secretly, I blamed myself for daring to dream such a bold dream of happiness. I was surrounded by people who had experienced similar disappointments in relationships; what did I truly expect in this situation? I planned to take corrective action and live more simply, live below the radar and not dream such big dreams about excellence and love, etc. One day, a trusted colleague approached me to share that they often noticed my struggles with doubt. From their perspective, it appeared that my speech was always doubtful. They shared that, in their experience, doubt only tended to cause unnecessary stress and suggested that I use my experiences to grow in my faith and increase efforts to achieve spiritual connectedness. That colleague was correct in their perceptions. Growing up, I attended Catholic school and went to church on Sundays and the holidays like many in our community. As I grew into adulthood and more independent, I found the act of leaning into prayer more satisfactory than the physical act of going to church. Even then, my prayer life felt empty and void of a true understanding of the power of prayer in our daily lives. It was my plan all along to move in this direction if only to gain control of all the internal emotional turbulence.

The book *The Purpose Driven Life* by Rick Warren came highly recommended. I read it immediately. Feeling a bit more inspired, once in a while, I would venture out to a local Bible study at a nearby church. I enjoyed them; they revealed a calmer, more logical approach to managing turbulence. Reading the Bible also demonstrated actionable steps for depending less on others and more on a direct relationship with God and the divine purpose that I was born to fulfill. The action steps to support my spiritual growth and healing increased exponentially that year. What I loved most about this was that what I needed to support my healing would often show up in friends, family, as well as friendly strangers, who always seemed to have the perfect advice for that time. To be clear, it isn't that this period was void of challenges, it's just that the challenges no longer seemed to drain me emotionally. Instead, whatever challenges there were took second place to a stronger emotional life force that was burgeoning through the seams. One such example was the decision to pursue my doctorate degree. I was encouraged by colleagues at work. I received six different pleas by three different individuals over the course of four years. They were clear about their recommendation; I should pursue a doctorate degree to support my career and further develop my talents. When I was first approached about continuing my education, I resisted. I always loved education, but I had set my mind on getting married and starting a family. My biological clock was ticking and there was this particular schedule I wanted to keep. Once I accepted the reality of the failed relationship, I started to contemplate my next steps. One colleague in particular would repeatedly plead with me, "But you love what you're doing AND you're good at it; having the doctorate will simply ensure that you solidify your voice within the professional space that you are working in." Emotionally, I finally freed myself to listen to those individuals who simply refused to give up on me or my career. I would formally enroll into a doctoral program later that year.

Like an early spring morning, the enrollment process felt fresh, life affirming, and far removed from any pain. These emotions associated with this new start felt different than when I had enrolled in college or the graduate-level program. Enrolling in those programs felt like an avenue to ensure my survival and a good paying job. In contrast, enrolling in the doctorate program felt like the door had opened to a new life of divine purpose that promised to be bold and adventurous. Ironically, this new life would also require more confidence and faith in myself, something that I had not prepared for. In hindsight, the sadness from all the disappointment made me want to enjoy a quieter life, void of any wishes to fulfill ambitious desires. Yet, spiritually, there was a very different plan emerging. The new plan was, by contrast, so bold that it would naturally move me toward greater visibility. This filled me with a different type of vision for happiness. Immediately following the start of school, I found myself exposed to a community of others who had either already completed their doctoral degree, were in the midst of pursuing it, or connected to others who were. The more my spiritual connectedness grew so too did my exposure to people who showed up to get me to the finish line. At the start of the second semester, my mentor simply walked into my life and introduced herself. We didn't know each other well but for the occasional on-campus meeting while working for the same institution. She became aware that I was pursuing my doctorate through others in our organization. She invited me to meet a group of other students like me whom she took an interest in mentoring. She indicated that the process was unfamiliar to anything we had ever experienced academically and would, therefore, require special mentorship. She further indicated that the statistics of those who started programs such as these but never completed them were so staggering she decided to do something about it by reaching back and providing mentorship. This, she explained, would be her way to give back. There was no perceived basis for this kindness; it simply arrived unannounced. More importantly, this kindness served me in ways that I needed for the entire length of the program, until the day that I graduated. In a somewhat similar fashion, on the first day of school I met two other students who were like-minded. During the first semester, our energies blended so well, we formed an agreement. The agreement was based on the fact that we started the program on the same day and had similar interests in Higher Education. The agreement required us to hold each accountable until all three of us completed the program. In fact, our motivational chant was, "We started together, were going to finish together." In keeping with our agreement, we would meet in person every weekend for six years straight, encouraging each other to successfully complete our requirements. Advice and support flowed freely among the three of us, always inspiring each other to keep our eyes on the finish line. Yet again, there was no perceived basis for this kindness; it happened naturally and served all of us well until the day we graduated from the program, together.

Chapter 7

It was no secret that the pursuit of my doctorate degree gave me a new lease on life. It gave me permission to experience the world through a different lens and create new expectations. I was clearer now that this new life adventure was going to lead to greater visibility and, therefore, require more social grace to maneuver as well as greater emotional strength. I needed to heal the places where I was too fragile, where I depended on others to dictate my emotions or moods. The soft places where I needed others to validate me made me feel accepted or that I belonged. I would simultaneously learn that my spiritual life could accomplish that goal like no other. Socially, I was challenged during the pursuit of this degree in ways that I would have never imagined. I was shocked by the nature of what events would regularly show up through the actions of others. I understood, however, that although these events presented themselves as adversity, their purpose was to strengthen, awaken, and mature my good senses. Adversity took on many practical forms but, most commonly, in the form of characters who came in and out of my life. They would do the exact opposite of providing validation or a safe place to belong. In fact, some arrived with actions that were downright threatening. The only difference was that I was now strong enough to embrace these actions, even appreciate them. Sharing the details of the individual stories would prove too complicated without the important background history to frame the narrative. Nonetheless, the opportunities they provided for broader learning are still accessible through the following examples.

The offended. The offended presented themselves in a variety of scenarios and tended to be quite upset with my decision to further my education. Their exact reason for their displeasure was never clear. The interactions were often confusing and subversively competitive. At times, I was even accused of actions that I had never done. Even more confusing was their announced concern for my well-being. Without warning, I found myself managing their sensitive emotions, while also trying to manage a completely different educational landscape. Exhausted, I decided that I wasn't going to apologize for investing in myself. I resolved that it was more about them than me. I also decided that if I had to choose between not offending them and investing in my education and my future, that I would always choose me and make peace with the consequences.

The friendly foe. The definition of the term friendly is someone who is pleasant, kind, and outgoing. The foe, on the other hand, is defined as an antagonist, rival, or competitor. The term friendly foe is therefore a contradiction, just like the person for whom this term is best utilized. The friendly foe had already existed in my environment. They were, up until the moment I discovered their true nature, individuals whom I enjoyed spending time with. As I came to understand the broad spectrum of the issue better, their outward contradictions were mostly due to personal challenges with self-worth that led them to hide deep emotional feelings of competition and antagonism. The potential for them to cause personal damage due to their ongoing competition was always a reality. As such, it's important to note that the level of damage a friendly foe can cause is in direct proportion to how much access you provide to your private thoughts. This competition, sadly, lives only within the deep valleys of their own minds and becomes emboldened by your desire to accomplish a goal. In an act of immature warfare, they might spread gossip or make up lies about you for the purpose of damaging your reputation. All while you stand by witnessing the state of this failing friendship, a friendship you once held dear. You might spend time wondering what could have happened and where exactly things took a wrong turn, only to realize that the only mistake you made was in assuming the friendship was based on a mutual bond of respect. Objectively speaking, if their complicated feelings could be addressed from a less antagonistic stance, you could explore the triggering behaviors together and encourage them to pursue their own goals. Unfortunately, this will not be the way of the friendly foe. Their actions will consistently betray their façade of friendship. Your only responsibility is to remain aware of how you feel and pay close attention to your instincts.

The obstructionist. One of the trickiest characters to navigate emotionally, it's not initially clear what the obstructionist is motivated by. What I learned, through years of exposure to and coexisting with obstructionists, was that the loss of control or appearance of such is a trigger. The obstructionist has the ability to play several different roles. A few examples include saboteur, project wrecker, or time waster; their goal seems to be to undermine the (*fill in the blank*) activity. Often, you're intermingled in some capacity either professionally or personally. You may even be dependent on their participation in something important to you. It won't be a secret that they're an obstructionist either because their communication tends to be harsh, harsher than is warranted for the situation. In addition, their destructive behavior may not be apparent to others around you, and any attempt to expose their behavior might place you in a vulnerable position. After doing some research on the topic, I decided I was going to turn the dynamic around by helping the obstructionists in my life feel more in control. I would work with them, fighting the feelings I had to work around them. I wanted to leave them out of conversations but, instead, trained myself to really hear their objections. I also trained myself to silence my own internal critic who really wanted to get back at them for being an obstructionist in the first place. Admittedly, through the objections of said obstructionists, I learned about the existence of valid concerns. Considered blind spots that needed to be addressed prior to the completion of (*fill in the blank*) activity. In reality, their concerns were merely communicated poorly and blocked what could have been an easier emotional process. By working together, we were forced to come up with alternative, creative solutions. Through practice and with time, I got better at this. Ironically, the hard work and effort I put into entertaining the obstructionist's concerns ultimately lessened their desire to be destructive.

The Critic. The critic seemed particularly judgmental about everything I did. They were also hyperfocused on my inability to participate in (*fill in the blank*) activity, irrespective of the fact that my time was now limited. Timewise, working full time while also going to school in the evenings and weekends was challenging. Despite doing my best to keep the pace with my responsibilities, the critic would use any opportunity to make me feel ashamed about not being present. It was all about them and their needs, so naturally, they took everything personal. My responsibilities, concerns, or difficulties weren't even factored into the equation. As I moved to prioritize my needs and downgrade their needs, the situation fell apart. It's true that there are some critics who mature beyond their circumstances and learn to work toward greater balance in their relationships. Others, however, may not be up for the challenge and decide to exit your life permanently. Though initially shocked, their exit provides room for those who are more aligned with you to enter your life. Consider it an even swap.

Emotionally, I did my best to learn as I moved through these experiences and relied on the only true source of security I had, my faith. I'm grateful for the educational opportunities they presented because the experiences facilitated some of the greatest development lessons I've learned. Through these experiences, I matured beyond my wildest dreams. Although I could have fought the lessons they needed to bring, I chose, instead, to embrace them and move calmly with their rhythm. I would eventually make peace with it all by thanking them for being exactly who they needed to be in those moments. Regardless, it's just as important to note that while the tough work of character development is facilitated through difficult characters, happily, strength is also developed through positive experiences demonstrated in the following examples.

Those Walking the Same Path. At times, we encounter those walking similar life paths. They seem to understand us more than most, simply because they're going through the exact same lessons within a certain timeframe. They're neither friend nor foe but provide a level of support that you might not have ever imagined possible. Their empathy can act as the exact type of nonjudgmental sounding board you need as you compare notes and encourage one another to keep going. This becomes increasingly important as your purpose requires more commitment.

The Fans. Last, but certainly not least are your fans. Your fans will be overjoyed by your progress in life and applaud each accomplishment. They are unflinching in their loyalty and remain uncompromising in their view of you as a positive life force. They'll cheer the positive outcomes as well as provide support during difficult times. These folks will reveal themselves to you slowly and will remain lifelong friends. Honor and cherish them without hesitation and with just as much loyalty as they've bestowed on you.

Chapter 8

THE PLAN WAS TO LIVE LIFE QUIETLY AND UNDER THE RADAR

The more that I experienced life's disappointments, the more questions I formulated about my purpose. I was in search of the answers to the riddle, the ones that would solve the mystery of these random nonsensical life events that I continuously found myself in. Sure, I learned the lessons they provided, but never understood their connection to my future. In response to all the confusion, I leaned into prayer. I felt connected spiritually but also knew that I needed more spiritual muscle. I struggled with persistent discouragement and was exhausted by the constant need to manage life's problems. Although prayer healed me, I felt compelled to incorporate more focused attention to the meaning of prayer as a way to access positive motivation and build strength. With each passing day, I was becoming more exposed to the type of nuances that were inconvenient and difficult to manage. It became clear that in order to learn from them, it might prove beneficial to journal them, review them at a later date when I had time to reflect, see them with a fresh perspective, and be less emotionally attached to their outcome. As I maneuvered through this challenging emotional landscape, I ultimately found what I was searching for through messengers. The first messenger was a childhood friend with whom I shared a similar frame of mind. It's true; we bonded over our perception of the world. We chose from an early age to see the world through a positive lens, despite our circumstances. We read a few highly recommended books that connected the dots between thought, speech, and manifestation. To summarize, we learned that a person's thoughts and speech have great power to shape the reality of their world. We compared notes on this philosophy and examined how it was showing up in our own lives. We also made a decision to hold each other accountable for sticking to positive frames of mind as well as speech during tough times. We would agree to lift each other up whenever we encountered challenges. We were both looking to access more joy, and this would be our path toward developing this important skill. The second messenger was someone else with whom I shared a close bond. In our company, you might be tempted to mistake us for sisters rather than friends. We had similar childhood experiences, so, emotionally, we spoke the same language. In our discussions, we explored the ways that we could walk in spiritual alignment with our desires and the many ways in which we needed to strengthen our commitment to better alignment. This propelled us, without hesitation, to change the very habits and practices that were hindering our progress. Yet again, there was a conscious decision to hold each other accountable and lean on each other during challenging times. Having acquired some strength and encouragement from the result of these prior efforts, the remaining answers would appear when I was in my own company. Frankly, for some of the complex issues I encountered, no one could help me with them. In addition, the fear of being judged for what I was feeling kept me emotionally isolated. But also, in this space, I developed the most authentic prayers. I committed myself to listening to my inner voice and tapping into my instincts. I prayed earnestly about what to do with anger, sadness, and disappointment. As a naturally optimistic person, I found it difficult to reconcile feelings of not wanting to deal with problems that seemed purposefully manufactured by others. They drained my optimistic spirit and energy. I felt powerless until I came to understand their deeper meaning. Surprisingly, anger, sadness, and disappointment also have a purpose. They simply cannot be avoided in life. They exist to remind us of our humaneness, connect us to others compassionately, or protect us from things that aren't meant for us. I began to notice that my instincts often delivered very precise messages, and all I needed to do was trust the message. During this time, I embraced the messages I received from within, there was indeed a divine plan for my life, and these challenges were there to prepare me to utilize what I had learned to help others.

The deeper truth about challenges in life is that we are more than the disappointments we experience. Hurt and pain simply cannot be avoided as a living breathing individual. Therefore, if we do what we can to escape feeling the pain of hurtful situations, we also avoid critical life lessons that need to be learned from those experiences. These lessons lead to necessary growth and have the power to assist with overcoming societal issues and becoming useful in our community.

Chapter 9

With little warning, I was offered an opportunity to advance in my career. It was the type of role that I had long dreamed of. I would pursue bold professional moves and assume greater levels of responsibility. Overnight, I found myself surrounded by new characters who didn't know my history or my trials. In an ironic twist, I felt as if I always belonged here. They were very welcoming and were even counting on me for guidance and expertise. They also showed great faith in my professional instincts. I had never experienced anything like this before. It felt so foreign; I often found myself doubting it. Deep down, however, I knew I was always searching for this. This demonstrative show of faith and confidence in me was the exact recipe for success I knew I could thrive in. So much so, that within one year, I was promoted into an even larger role with greater responsibility. Two months following my promotion, I would complete my doctoral degree. As a testament to increased faith and spiritual muscle, the day before I would defend my dissertation, I experienced a major challenge. Defending one's dissertation is considered the last step in completing graduation requirements toward the doctoral degree, which necessitates an in-person oral presentation. The day before the defense, the snowfall was so heavy there was a threat of closure on the campus and building where I was scheduled to deliver the defense. If the defense were to be cancelled, that would mean waiting another six months to defend and possibly another year to graduate. I didn't panic or become anxious. Internally, I laughed at the irony and prayed through the storm. I even visited a local coffee shop, regardless of the threat of snow accumulation, to practice my presentation. I seemed to be that sure that all would be well. The next day, I would defend my dissertation on the sunniest winter day. The sun was warm and melted the snow outside, but my joy filled the hallways inside. It felt incredibly empowering like running a marathon, completing the race, and showing up to collect my medal. It was a grueling process, but I had proven to myself that I was both capable and strong. One month after that, I would deliver the commencement speech at a famous theater to a crowd of more than a thousand. The crowd consisted of a class of graduating seniors and their families and friends. I simply practiced my presentation and delivered. I had come full circle, evolving, growing, and pushed out onto the world stage. The lights of the theater shined brightly in my direction as the world and my colleagues watched.

The fast pace and rapid succession of these accomplishments in this short time overwhelmed my senses. I got the distinct sense that this was just the beginning. There were important professional goals I desired to materialize. The opportunities were finally here, and they were real. My only task now was to get comfortable in this new skin.

Chapter 10

The range of professional opportunities ahead of me was limitless. It would be up to me to define the shape of my future, and I was thrilled about that. I wanted to develop a framework for the purpose of the struggle and then assign it meaning that could resonate with others and assist others who had been through similar trials. Why else would I have gone through all of this, I thought? I was fascinated by what was waiting to be uncovered. I reflected back on a specific chapter I read in *The Purpose Driven Life*. There was heavy emphasis on connecting one's gifts to one's life path. It felt as if the timing was right for diving deeper into this lens. Up until now, I had only perceived prayer as the vehicle I needed to keep me encouraged in the face of adversity. I had not yet connected the greater meaning of the total experience as a vehicle that could serve others. This was, indeed, what I was searching for. Greater expansion tended to bring new problems to solve. Therefore, greater wisdom is needed to find appropriate solutions and access more meaning for managing the journey. Once again, I would be assisted through messengers dressed as lifelong friends who were also searching for greater meaning. Without hesitation, we discussed how we might encourage each other through a process of discovery, discipline, and worship. Personally, what I was searching for were ways to manage my emotions, my reactions to disappointment and challenging individuals. I also longed to better understand why or how these challenges found their way to my doorstep, especially since I wasn't seeking them. Through consistent discipline, I learned that no matter how difficult the situation, prayer could assist with arriving at a resolution. No longer would I fear the arrival of difficult times, I would use them instead as a vehicle to strengthen my approach to life. This helped me to detach from anxiety and the criticisms of others. I felt stronger at my core and incredibly empowered. Without a doubt, furthering my education provided the tools I needed to excel in my profession; however, the tools that were most useful for overcoming emotional challenges were through my disciplined prayer life. I now understood that I needed them both on my journey to the next level. This profound shift in understanding revolutionized my daily activities. As a whole, I experienced increased focus and discipline, the groundwork for getting more of my goals accomplished. There was also a corresponding social transition. I refrained from getting into unnecessary conflict or conversations that had no hope of resolution by simply identifying them in advance. I also seemed to be listening better to my surroundings, to my instincts, as well as to others. What was revealed through all this listening was how much people lived in fear of their potential and the potential of others. Consequently, I learned to better understand how to soothe the fears of others through compassion and compromise. The focus shifted from myself to meeting the needs of others and challenges head on. My world was now brimming with constant excitement and experiencing more joy from everything that was converging to support my goals.

Following graduation, my family and friends gathered for a graduation party. It was a wonderful celebration and felt surreal to view my future through this lens. I had now accumulated many years of experience teaching health professional students. Within the learning environment, I often encouraged students to think deeper about the challenges their future patients would face. The students I taught, the same ones preparing to provide care for the broader population, in some instances, weren't ready for the nuances of the healthcare system. Through my experiences in the learning environment, I had also come to understand the challenges in the area of recruitment and retention of students underrepresented in healthcare. With the expansion of my professional role, it was time to demonstrate to the world what exactly I understood about this topic that was so different from anyone else who dedicated their life's work to this. Most importantly, I reflected on what I would do differently with that knowledge to make a noticeable difference in the lives of others. I would use this framework to define my professional future and, more importantly, plan a social life filled with more joy.

Chapter 11

THE PLAN WAS TO STOP MAKING PLANS

I had made up my mind. It was time to start living life with more vigor as I integrated all the valuable lessons from the prior years. Difficult people and life challenges were no longer as scary as they used to be. I had some tools under my belt and was feeling more confident overall. Life was going so well it seemed only right that I abandon this fascination that I had with making plans. I had this habit of taking my plans too seriously and if life decided to change the direction of those plans, I would become incredibly upset. *Plans,* I thought, *were only a set up for more disappointment and facilitated mental torture if they failed.* So, I decided it was time to say goodbye to making plans and the empty promises they brought with them. I would set myself free for good.

It was a bright sunny day in the month of June. I was on my way to work and had already received five missed calls. This never happened, so whatever it was, it was an emergency. I didn't hesitate to call back as soon as I could secure an internet connection. It was worse than I could have ever imagined. The inevitable had happened, a crisis of epic proportions that could potentially threaten my future and everything I associated with it. An investigation would follow, months of intense work and concentration to clear the professional debris. Through it all, I persisted with what I had learned from all my prior tribulations: prayer, positivity, and purpose. I laid bare my fears and once again resolved that whatever the resolution, it was going to strengthen me in unimaginable ways. It wasn't until this particular incident that I came to understand the divine wisdom of my prior trials. Without those lessons I might not have been able to maneuver through this with the calm that I needed to. So much so, a colleague thanked me for showing up daily with a steady calm demeanor during a truly nerve-racking time of professional intrigue. I considered this further proof of just how far I had come. Emotionally, I was being prepared, unbeknownst to me, for this particular challenge. As the months progressed, everyone contributed to working as hard as they could to succeed through the difficulties. One day, a new directive arrived via email. It was clear, precise, and had a strict timeline. We were tasked with creating a strategic plan. The plan would have to be detailed and incorporate each departmental map for effectively meeting our goals in five years. Furthermore, planning would have to start effective immediately.

The end

Acknowledgements

I owe the development of this book to the many experiences and individuals I encountered along the way. I'm eternally grateful for their contributions to my growth.

References

1. Clay, W. et al (2021) Does the AAMC's Definition of "Underrepresented in Medicine" Promote Justice and Inclusivity? *AMA Journal of Ethics, 23*(12), E960-964.
2. Bolger, N. et al (2000). Invisible support and adjustment to stress. *Journal of Personality and Social Psychology, 79*, 953-961
3. Spiegel, D. et al. (1989). Effect of psychosocial treatment on survival of patients with metastatic breast-cancer. *Lancet, 2*, 888- 891.
4. Baumeister, R., & Leary, M. (1995). The need to belong: Desire for interpersonal attachments as a fundamental human motivation. *Psychological Bulletin, 117(3)*, 497-529.
5. MacDonald, G., & Leary, M. (2005). Roles of social pain and defense mechanisms in response to social exclusion: Reply to Panksepp (2005) and Corr (2005). *Psychological Bulletin, 131*, 237-240
6. Mahoney, J. L., & Cairns, R. B. (1997) Do Extracurricular Activities Protect against Early School Dropout? *Developmental Psychology, 33*, 241-253. http://dx.doi.org/10.1037/0012-1649.33.2.241
7. Brown, A. L., & Campione, J. C. (1998). Designing a community of young learners: Theoretical and practical lessons. In N. M. Lambert & B. L. McCombs (Eds.), *How students learn: Reforming schools through learner-centered*

education (pp. 153–186). American Psychological Association. https://doi.org/10.1037/10258-006
8. Caprara, G. V. et al. (2000). Prosocial foundations of children's academic achievement. *Psychological Science, 11*, 302 - 306.
9. Cohen, G. & Steele, C. (2002). A barrier of mistrust: How stereotypes affect cross-race mentoring. In J. Aronson (Ed.), *Improving academic achievement: Impact of psychological factors on education* (pp. 305–331). Academic Press.

Author Biography

Dr. Nadege Dady is an experienced educator with a terminal degree in Higher Education, Leadership, Management and Policy. Her ever-expansive career covers a range of health care sectors. These collective experiences in the allopathic, osteopathic, and oral health care industries have only fueled her passions for creating pathway programs for underrepresented groups in medicine. Adding to her broad range of experiences are consulting with the accrediting agencies responsible for medical school regulatory practices and editing for a medical journal.

Through this book, she seeks to encourage the positive development of others and to push the reader beyond fear or hopelessness toward the successful management of the everyday challenges we face.

URGENT PLEA!

Thank You For Reading My Book!

I really appreciate all of your feedback and
I love hearing what you have to say.

Please take two minutes now to leave a helpful review on Amazon, letting me know what you thought of the book:

https://www.amazon.com/dp/B0CBKZ6RJ9?ref_=cm_sw_r_mwn_dp_8T2QRY15SRC0XZ5A0329

Thanks so much!
Nadege Dady, Ed.D.

www.ingramcontent.com/pod-product-compliance
Lightning Source LLC
Chambersburg PA
CBHW071228160426
43196CB00012B/2448